# SELL!
# SELL!
# SELL!

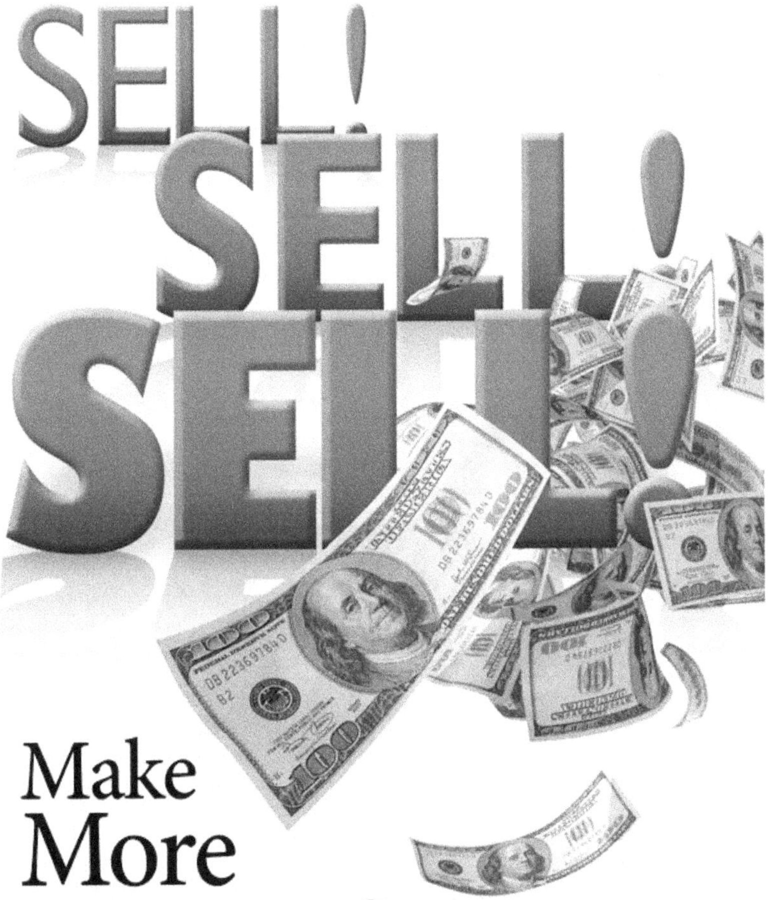

# Make
# More
# Money!

Rick Edwards

# Sell! Sell! Sell!
## Make More Money!

**A Rick Edwards Book**
Copyright © 2010, Rick Edwards
All rights reserved.

Book Cover created and designed by Tracey Miller (*www.TraceOfStyle.com*).

Edited by Lauren Cullumber & Published by Weston Lyon (*www.PlugAndPlayPublishing.com*).

ISBN:1456357948

EAN-13: 978-1456357948

# Sell! Sell! Sell!
## Table of Contents

# Introduction

**Why I Chose Sales for a Living**
Growing up in the family business in the home remodeling industry, I knew at a young age what I wanted to do. Selling was a 'trade' in my family and I knew that not everyone 'qualified' for the trade. The business of sales was in my blood and all around me.

In business, without sales, nothing happens!

The way I saw it, salespeople always seemed to be making the most money and having the most fun. They also seemed to be a support team for each other; as well as the drivers of the business – bringing in the revenue (and making sure everyone else had a job).

**Why a Book on Sales?**
We've all seen how frustrating the sales role can be for the new salesperson, or the experienced person when they're not selling well or they go into a slump.

My role as a sales trainer and manager has given me the luxury of knowing how to teach simple steps to selling. I can test the trainee for comprehension, then get them back on track and help keep them there. I enjoy sharing the structure that has given me the confidence to know that no matter what happens with the economy or the marketplace, I can always make money selling. In some instances, I've been able to take an experienced salesperson and double his productivity in one week of training.

Also, I have had the privilege of building a $30M sales organization of forty-five salespeople, one trainee at a time.

I hope you realize that I say this not to impress you. Rather I want to impress upon you that a book on the sales system, this book, is exactly what is needed... and I'm the person to show you the way.

**What Makes a Successful Salesperson?**
What does a successful salesperson look like? How do they think? How do they act? What exactly do they do that makes them so successful?

Many people who enter the field of sales feel or have been told that they are a natural for it. They've been told they are "good talkers" or really smart and quick or creative thinkers.

Well, after making literally thousands of sales calls, and working with hundreds of sales representatives over the years, I've seen what it takes to be a successful sales representative.

In my opinion, successful salespeople have these three traits in common:

1. **They have a positive, enthusiastic attitude** - Attitude and enthusiasm are the main ingredients of successful sales. The power of positive thinking is an amazing thing. If you believe you can do something, you can. Successful sales start here.

2. **They are "good listeners"** - Successful salespeople ask open-ended questions and listen completely to the answers, remembering what they've heard and using those answers (the prospect's own words) to help close sales.

3. **They use a structured sales approach** - Successful salespeople guide the prospects through a systematic presentation that gives the prospect information and ideas, which allows them to be comfortable about moving forward right away. All this allows them to close the sale with ease, asking for the order in a way that their prospects are comfortable making a commitment and moving ahead.

In addition, successful salespeople are good storytellers. Some say, "It's all in the story!" They know how to use their words to build rapport, capture the audience's attention, and make them laugh. Telling stories not only sets people at ease, it helps you sell more. Remember, facts tell; stories sell!

## Why This Book?

Unfortunately, most people will always do what they've always done. You are reading this, so maybe you are the unique one who is ready for a positive change.

This book has been written as a detailed reference for sales training. This is a no-nonsense, systematic approach to selling that has been proven to work thousands of times.

Maybe you work for a company that has no structured sales presentation. Imagine moving yourself to number one in your company or in your industry!

Please read it thoroughly and study all of the information presented.

There is a tremendous amount of information included in this book. I recommend you write, rewrite and memorize your own presentation, not to give a canned presentation, but to make it your own.

You are encouraged to take notes and/or highlight any part in this book to aid in your comprehension.

This book is designed to assist you in your selling success. If you have any questions or comments regarding its content or format, please feel comfortable to share your ideas by e-mail (or visit www.sellsellsellbook.com).

Good luck!

*Rick Edwards*

**PS** - So many people in the sales role are working really hard at the job and are not making the type of money they deserve. Their earnings could increase dramatically simply by conveying the information to their sales prospects in a way that makes their buying decision easy.

This book is written in such a way as to simplify the process for the salesperson and make more sales.

**51% of sales are likeability and trust. This book contains the other 49%.**

# Getting Started

Welcome to the world of structured sales. This book
has been designed to assist you in getting on track in
your sales career. In this section, we'll look at: The
Basics of Selling and Your Own Job Description
(what you do and are expected to do).

## Learning the Basics

The basics of successful selling haven't changed much
through the years. Whether it's face to face or over
the phone, by utilizing a selling structure, selling can
be easy, predictable and lots of fun.

A selling structure puts YOU in control. It has been
proven that when a professional selling structure is
utilized, you have a huge advantage over the competition and can sell your products or services for more
money and frequently, on the first visit.

Using a selling structure, you can predict almost exactly what will happen next (and next and next)
throughout your sales presentation.

Using a selling structure, you're the master; it's like
playing a game of cards, chess or checkers with someone who is new at the game (you play it every day,
and they may have never played at all).

Before your presentation even starts, you will know what will happen next and then you'll know how your prospect will respond to it.

You'll know how to create your presentation to minimize objections at the end of the process (the close) and you'll know the automated responses to each excuse or objection you'll encounter during the close.

In other words, you'll know how to overcome their excuses and objections in a way that will lead you down the path of closing the sale.

Finally, you'll learn how to button-up the sale to prevent your sale from canceling; as well as how to get your new customer to offer you referrals, immediately.

Now, the only way to succeed is to plan for it. Each day is your own and you can work as hard as you like - depending on your income goals.

Remember, having the basics of a selling system down pat can make your income more predictable – in any economy!

**Selling is Your Responsibility**
Selling is your responsibility, no one else's. Successful salespeople not only survive, they thrive in almost

any environment. So, while your employer may have a successful marketing plan and may keep you busy most of the time, it is up to you to have a plan to keep yourself making money on your own.

Create a pattern for your own success every day.

Here are 16 habits that I've developed over the years for myself. They work for me...read them and figure out how they can work for you, too:

**1.** Start early
**2.** Be prepared for a slow day
**3.** Teach others
**4.** Learn from others
**5.** Ask for opinions and advice from the pros
**6.** Plan for success
**7.** Market yourself
**8.** Make people feel special
**9.** Set goals
**10.** Track your goals
**11.** Master your presentation
**12.** Smile!
**13.** Make *them* feel special
**14.** Be enthusiastic
**15.** Be a consultant
**16.** Be a closer

Again, these habits have worked for me and can work for you, as well. Use them as a guide to develop your own basic success habits.

Remember, habits take time to develop. Keep this list in front of you every day and read it before you go to work. Consistency is key.

**Your Own Job Description**
As a professional sales representative, or if you own or manage a business that employs professional sales representatives, it is extremely important to have a complete written job description.

Your job description should go something like this:
- Begin each day at a 'specific time'
- Review lead results from the previous day
- Build a database of prospects and previous customers
- Send thank you cards to customers from the previous day
- Focus on new appointments for the current day
- Plan current marketing efforts, work existing customers and referrals
- Generate referrals and canvass appointments
- Possess a professional knowledge of your products and your competition
- Advance your education during times when leads are slow by riding with others and visiting customers

- Follow up immediately on all paperwork and promises made to customers

Nothing fancy here. Just a written expectation of what needs to be done. By having a job description mapped out, you add structure and accountability to the sales role.

This is extremely important for measuring expectations, for you and/or your coworkers or employees. And, when you have crystal clear expectations, you can inspect them and enforce them, if necessary. No structure and no accountability are a recipe for disaster (*i.e. – you making no money*)!

So, using the above list, as well as some ideas of your own, write YOUR job description. What do you do? What are you expected to do?

Start here and expand as needed. Remember, success is up to you, so your description of what's expected is your foundation. A solid foundation is critical. Build your foundation now:

_____

_____

_____

_____

_____

_____

# Your Selling Structure

Before we move into the heart of this book, I think some definitions will help:

*Sales:* A conveyance of ideas.

*Salesperson:* One whose job or career is to convey ideas to others.

*Professional Salesperson:* One who has a belief in utilizing a proven systematic process of conveying ideas in a way to consistently motivate others to purchase his or her products or services.

The whole point of you reading this book is to become a professional salesperson.

Isn't it time to make consistent sales? Isn't it time to make this job predictable? Isn't it time to make more money? If you answered YES to these questions, then you need a selling structure.

A selling structure offers a systematic process leading to consistent success in closing sales. The process systematically educates the prospect and offers the information that allows the prospect to comfortably move forward and invest in you and what you are selling.

By using an easy to learn selling structure, I've enjoyed the role of salesperson, had a tremendous amount of fun, made thousands of new friends and made way more money than I ever imagined.

Also, in building a sales organization, and hiring and training hundreds of salespeople to do a structured sales presentation, I came to understand that a structured selling plan allows new hires to get trained more quickly.

When using a structured system, managers and trainers can evaluate their presentation and identify mistakes that are being made in the field, and then repair their presentation for maximum success, fast!

When potential sales are being missed, it means the person has changed what he was doing when he was successful and must be retrained. He only has to get back to the system to be successful again.

What does this mean for you? Putting a structured sales process in place - and making mid-course corrections to perfect it along the way - can give you a secure, predictable income that can be scaled up or down depending on your goals. And the really cool part is: when you have a system that works for you, you can identify if something goes wrong immediately!

So, if you ever get into a slump, just observe where in the system you got off track and get back on track. Sales will increase automatically...because it's the system that works!

Understand we're only human. We get off track occasionally and can be easily distracted. Focus on your system and success is yours for the taking.

**Writing a Selling Structure**
Your presentation must be different than your competition. Doing this is simple. Maybe you've heard of a 5-step, 8-step or 10-step presentation.

This is simply a methodic way to present the information, a requirement to make your prospect comfortable about moving forward with you, your company and products.

By writing out and possessing your own selling system, you can "convey the ideas" that will build your success and consistently close sales –
remember, you're a professional!

The following is a list of the steps that we use in our industry (and that I'm going to discuss with you throughout the rest of this book).

**Steps to a Sale:**
1. Marketing Yourself
2. Entry: Initiate Your Presentation
3. Warm-Up: Make Friends, Establish Trust
4. Survey/Assessment: Determine Buying Habits, Assess Needs, Prevent Objections
5. Your Company Story: What Makes Your Company "Better"?
6. Setting the Stage: Recap: Restate Urgency
7. Your Product: Demonstration
8. Delivering the Price
9. Closing the Sale
10. Post Close

# Step 1
## Marketing Yourself

# Step 1: Marketing Yourself

Marketing (or getting leads) is the starting point of any successful selling process. You must work to become your own marketing department. Become a celebrity at what you do.

Now, while I admit I'm no expert in all facets of marketing, here are 4 easy-to-implement marketing ideas to help you get started:

   1. **Business cards:** Pass out your business cards to everyone you meet, like they're going out of style.

The average person knows about 200 people. Most people know people like themselves, so there are prospects all around you.

   2. **Personal website:** Websites are simple and cheap to build these days. Go to a domain host website like <u>GoDaddy.com</u>, find a domain name that suits your business or profession, and market yourself.

   3. **Social media:** Facebook is an ideal place to market. Today people are looking for your Facebook page to learn more about you, your family and friends.

By sending a message about your products or career that is interesting enough to receive a response, your message could reach thousands...and it's free!

**4. Networking:** There are dozens of industry trade networks and networking groups, Rotary, Chambers of Commerce and general business networking groups.

While marketing yourself and becoming your own marketing department, here are some important factors to keep in mind:

- Work your company's current or previous customers for referrals. Your company may have hundreds or even thousands of satisfied customers. These customers deserve to know you, they know people like themselves and everyone is eager to help! Remember, "Much is lost by not asking."

- Keep good records. On a slow day, you'll want to follow up with previous customers or rehash (contact prospects that didn't sell). The more information you have in front of you, the more success you'll see.

- Set goals, track results, and compete with yourself. This week, compete with last week. This month, compete with last month.

- Track your goals: prospect contacts, canvassing numbers, appointments, presentations, sales, and retention. Make reports daily, weekly, monthly, and yearly. Without goals, you're lost.
- Maintain your contacts, they're a valuable asset.
- Make more appointments! More appointments equal more sales and more money.

This is not an exhaustive list! There are more ways and more factors to keep in mind when marketing yourself and your business.

This is a topic I highly recommend you seeking out, and learning all you can about. Once you have your sales system in place (which you will by the end of this book), ramping up the marketing becomes numero uno on your list. After all, the more people you get in front of (using your system), the more sales you make and the easier this all becomes.

**Setting Appointments**
Appointments should be set using a script. Many of the things you say and the points you make during your presentation should be said word for word each time. When you communicate this way, most people will understand what is being said most of the time.

If people are misunderstanding what you are trying to say, time is being wasted and sales (your money) are lost. The following is a good word for word script for setting a confirmed appointment:

*"What I would like to do is set up a time when I can catch both you and all the interested parties together. I'll take a look at what you have in mind and I'll show both of you my products.*

*While I'm there I can give you a price quote on the project – no obligation. It'll only cost you a cup of coffee!"* (Make it sound quick and simple and fun!)

*"Are you ever both there during the daytime?"* (Try for the more difficult daytime appointment time slots first.)

*"Is Tuesday or Wednesday better? Which is better: 10:00AM or 2:00PM?"* ('Choice-close' the appointment: This gives them two choices and "assumes" the appointment and prevents them from saying no regarding an appointment.)

*"What is your first name? OK. And your husband's/wife's/partner's name?"* (Always get the names of all of the interested parties.)

*"Great! I'll see you both there Tuesday at 6:00 PM. If
something comes up please call, otherwise I'll see you
and _____ then."* (Confirm the day and time to
ensure you're both on the same page.)

This might go against your gut reaction, but you may
find that when an appointment is more difficult to
set, it is often easier to sell once you are there. So,
don't get discouraged. It's time to go make some
money.

## Preparation

In just a moment, we're going to being exploring the
'presentation' part of your system. Keep the following
in mind while preparing for your face-to-face meeting.

Make a complete sales presentation. Your presentation will be designed and refined to address all of the
concerns of most customers and to list all of the benefits of doing business with you and your company.

Making a complete presentation is like playing poker
and holding four aces. You have a winning hand.
Don't discard any of the aces; you never know when
you will need all of them to win.

It is essential that you include each element every
time. The presentation must be your own. It must be
your style, flair, humor, personality and confidence.

This can only be achieved through practice. Work with the presentation and memorize it until you feel it is yours, then present it completely every time.

In addition, when setting up an appointment, and while on an appointment, here are some important tips to make your day and career more successful:

- Always be meticulously on time for every appointment. When you start your presentation with an apology for being late, and the prospect doesn't have the time to listen to your complete presentation, or they have a negative attitude because you were late, sales are lost.

- Be optimistic and enthusiastic. Your attitude is everything.

- Set a fast pace.

- Don't waste their time.

- Don't waste your time.

- Always set appointments with all decision-makers present.

- Set appointments as soon as possible, within 48 hours, if possible, while the interest level is high.

- Confirm the appointment when set: "I'm very prompt, so I'll see you at 3 o'clock on Tuesday; if something comes up please give me a call, otherwise I'll see you (or both of you) then."

# Step 2
## The Entry

# Step 2: The Entry

The Entry is the starting point of any good selling presentation. This is where any necessary preparations must take place. It is also at this point that the true sales person takes charge.

You must have control of the selling situation if you expect to have any chance of making the sale. There are many things that can be required to take control of a situation. The following are the most important:

♦ Gaining Entry
♦ Having ALL Decision Making Parties Present
♦ Getting the Customer into a Decision Making Area
♦ Eliminating Distractions
♦ Controlling the Time Allotment

Two Key Factors to a Successful Entry that You Must Never Forget:
   **1.** Attitude and Enthusiasm
   **2.** Do not prejudge a lead, neighborhood or home-owner. Remember...they invited you...they want what you are selling and have verified already that they are interested. You will find many surprises.

GAINING ENTRY is usually not difficult. However, there are times when a salesperson is turned away without ever getting into the appointment. This is rarely a problem if the appointment is set properly; your customers know you are scheduled to visit and they are expecting you.

**Basic Rules:**

- Knock on the door; don't ring the bell. Strangers ring, friends knock. And, knocking won't wake small children.
- Back away from the door so you don't startle them.
- Use their names twice before using your own. *"Thank you for having me out, Robert. This is a beautiful home (or nice office, place of business) you have here, Robert."* Say this clearly to BOTH if there are two parties.

**Your Objective:**
To find the kitchen table or the place (conference table) where they likely do their business.

Occasionally, a customer will meet the salesperson and resist letting us inside. In our industry, suggesting a "walk around" and beginning the Warm Up (next step) while still outside can overcome this.

A statement should be made on the order of, *"We have many different things we can do for you...let's go in where we can get comfortable and I can show you what we have to offer."*

Do not do a presentation on a car or porch. You are not in control and have almost no chance of making the sale.

If you do the walk around with just the first prospect and a second prospect (another interested party) comes into the setting, you must review everything that was discussed outside once you are inside with the other party to make sure that they feel as though they are an important part of this presentation.

If you fail to do this you will lose them during the presentation - they will excuse themselves and get up and leave - because they feel that this presentation is between you and the other party.

Always start by thanking the customer for having you out. Then introduce yourself and comment on how nice the home is. *"This is a beautiful home (or place of business) you have here!"* should be your very first statement to both.

If you say it to one when the other is not present, be sure to say it to the other once they are.

Next, ask, *"How long have you lived here (or been in business)?"* Your interest will get you off on the right foot.

HAVING ALL DECISION-MAKING PARTIES PRESENT is mandatory. Most decisions are NOT the domain of only one party no matter what the customer may say.

We usually do not do a presentation on a "one leg" appointment (when all interested parties are not present). To do so will always result in the customer saying that they will talk to the other party and call you back.

The policy, if you are faced with a one-legged appointment, is to do a warm-up, generate interest and survey the customer that is present on the project; then reset the appointment when all interested parties will be there.

Usually, by saying you'll bring more information or pricing you'll encounter little resistance. In reality, you're coming back to do a full presentation and make a sale!

The time to find out about other interested parties is during the "ENTRY" part of the visit. Following up on the missing party's absence is necessary at this time.

If the other party is due to return shortly, the warm up can be prolonged. If they are not expected, warm up, build interest, and offer to come back with more information then set another appointment when both parties will be present.

GETTING THE CUSTOMER INTO A DECISION-MAKING AREA means exactly what it implies. Most important decisions made in the home are made around the kitchen table. Therefore, it is best to get the customer sitting at the table before beginning the actual sales presentation.

This is not always possible, but is a big enough plus for the representative that the attempt to move the customer from the den or living room to the kitchen should be made.

The best way to take control at this point is to tell the customer that we have something "new, exciting and different" to show them. Sometimes these require a table, and suggest, in question form, moving to the kitchen while at the same time getting up and leading the customer into the area desired.

ELIMINATING DISTRACTIONS is very important. A customer watching TV cannot give the representative his/her full attention. Small children who cause disturbances interfere with the sales presentation.

The same applies to a customer that will not stay with the presentation. Fortunately, these situations are often easy to correct using the silence is golden theory. Whenever one of these problems arises, the smart salesperson will stop mid-sentence and stay quiet until the disturbance is resolved. After several such stoppages, the customer will realize that the salesperson needs their full attention. If you continue speaking at a very soft level this can also resolve most distractions.

CONTROLLING THE TIME ALLOTMENT for the presentation is an important factor in successful selling. A quality sales presentation may take from one and one-half to two and one-half hours (do not tell the customer this!). Some products or services take less time.

People are busy; never let your customer feel like you are wasting their time. If presented with a deadline that cannot be met, suggest resetting the appointment for a more convenient time. Then get out of the home as graciously as possible.

If presented with an acceptable deadline or one that can be stretched, follow the selling steps and make a complete presentation.

# Step 3

## Warm-up

# Step 3: Warm-up

Your warm up starts when you arrive; conduct a sincere and thorough warm up with every customer.

Warming up doesn't mean engaging in senseless chatter, or asking a string of meaningless questions. The most successful salespeople are those who are sincere about helping customers. Find out why the customer is interested in your products and assure them that you can help.

Always be aware of your surroundings and ask the customer questions about what you observe. You are likely to see things like trophies, pictures or a fishing boat in the driveway. If so, chances are that someone likes to fish and probably enjoys talking about it. Ask open-ended questions and let your customers do most of the talking. They are usually more interested in telling their stories than in listening to yours.

Don't be phony; if you don't enjoy fishing, don't pretend you do. Rather, ask them what they enjoy about it. <u>Make them feel special</u>.

Be sure to set a fast pace in the warm up to prevent them from feeling that your visit is going to take too much time. There is a sales strategy called 'pacing' which is to mimic the customer's pace or 'tone', not to imitate but to make the customer comfortable feeling he is dealing with someone like himself. This is a perfect time to offer a gift.

A small gift will turn even the most difficult prospect into a friend and improve your chances of having their attention throughout your presentation. There are lots of marketing specialties available such as private label window cleaner, coffee mugs and special refrigerator magnets that are dry erase or message boards.

If the prospect offers something to eat or drink, I recommend that you take it. This makes them comfortable by being a good host and making you more comfortable. This is an important step in making friends, which is critical for you to gain the trust necessary to help them.

### Information Gathering
The first thing that you want to do when you pull into the neighborhood is looking for the inevitable bad projects that are near your customer's home. You might be able to make reference to them in your presentation.

When you arrive at your customer's home, look for good things that you can say about your customer's property. Look for landscaping or gardens, boats, campers, mountain bikes, basketball goals and most importantly, recent home improvements. Your goal when you get to the door is to get into the home and make a great first impression.

You want to warm up inside the den or family room. The den is usually the trophy room. Look for pictures of sons/daughters in the military, scholastic awards, trophies, etc. The things that they are proud of will be prominently displayed.

**Warm up with both of your customers.** The one that you don't involve in all the aspects of your presentation is the one that will kill your sale. Talk about their interests. Let them do most of the talking. Your customer will enjoy telling stories more than he will enjoy listening to yours. Smile and relax while asking open-ended questions, then listen completely to the answers.

Rapport is a valuable selling tool. Since the average person today knows about 200 people and those people also know 200 people, there is a chance that your prospects know someone that you know.

By *finding out where they are originally from, where they went to school, what they do for a living and where they work* you are likely to hit on someone or something that you have in common.

**The last thing we talk about in the warm up is business.** The idea here is to let everyone relax a little and let the customer get to know and like you.

The best way we have found to accomplish this is to let the customer talk about himself or his family. You need to ask questions that will allow them to do this.

At the same time, you can be gathering information about your customer. This information will help you plan your strategy on what adjustments will be needed to enhance your chances of turning this into a sale.

Always remember to *listen* to your customer. If they want to talk, let them, and listen. The customer will tell you exactly how to sell him.

Don't forget, it's ok to have fun. LAUGHTER IS A VERY IMPORTANT INGREDIENT IN SUCCESS. You will find that the most successful sales professionals do the best warm-up.

The following lists are highlights to read now and re-read on a regular basis. Internalizing these points is vital to your success in sales...as a professional salesperson.

## 51% OF SALES IS LIKEABILITY and TRUST

- Compliment the home, focus on them
- Make them feel special
- Put your problems aside, smile and be a good listener
- Relax them
- Do not 'expect' them to make a decision
- Your presentation is to educate them
- Price estimate will not be today only
- Look them in the eye
- Remember their names and repeat them often
- Start your presentation in terms of "if" and "when"
- Don't talk too much about yourself; their favorite subject is them

### Best Topics to Discuss in Your Warm Up

- How long have they owned their home?
- Where are they originally from?
- How did they meet?
- Mr.'s Employment, "*What type of work do you do?*"
- Mrs.'s Employment (Don't leave her out, and no-one is just a housewife.)
- Children/Grandchildren?
- Hobbies (Any trophies displayed?)
- Motorcycles, Boats, Campers, Etc.
- Who does the maintenance and when was it done last?

- How long do they plan on staying in their home?
- Place of worship
- Where the children go to school
- Pets

## ADVANTAGES OF A GOOD WARM UP

- Customers are relaxed
- Sales resistance is lowered
- Customers like you
- Customers begin to trust you
- You: Become more relaxed, have more information, begin to read the customer better, and have enhanced your chances for a sale

When you decide to make the transition from WARM UP to the SURVEY, your survey form should be handy along with a brochure and whatever other forms and literature that you use.

You have already acquired some of the information so just confirm and write it in. The use of the following two key questions will help you:

**1. How did you hear about my company?**
Depending on the answer to the first question, the follow up question would be...

## 2. Why have you decided to take care of this project now?

Listen, but understand that it really does **<u>not</u>** matter what the answers are...now you are talking business.

Now you can seamlessly transition into your survey.

# Step 4

## Survey

# Step 4: Survey

A written survey is the best way to collect information required to evaluate needs, budget and preferences. Design your own survey form using the concept presented in this section.

In selling real estate, it would be important to know the area, size and style of home, and their budget to ensure that time is not wasted showing properties that are unsuitable. Likewise, in other industries, a survey can establish the type of product, time line and budget to help save time and maximize results.

**Note**: To prevent the customers from being defensive about answering these questions, use the story of why realtors do their surveys to evaluate needs and budgets so they offer better service by having that information first and explain, "This prevents them from showing the wrong types of properties."

Most importantly, if done properly will prevent certain objections such as "time line," "need to talk with someone else (friend, family member, expert) before making a decision," "payment is too high," "we may sell the home," "we have another project that is more important" or "we're not going to move forward at this time."

If they refuse to answer any of the questions or get defensive don't be concerned, just move forward.

## MAIN INFORMATION GATHERING QUESTIONS TO ASK DURING THE SURVEY:

**1.** How did you hear about my company?

**2.** How do you plan to use your new product?

**3.** How long have you been thinking about it?

**4.** Do you know anyone that has purchased this product?

**5.** Is it ours or someone else's?

**6.** Have you seen something in the marketplace that you like?

**7.** Why do you need the product, how do you plan to use it?

**8.** What has held you back to this point?

**9.** Why have you decided to take care if it now?

**10.** Have you had any other projects like this done in the past few years?

**11.** What else (or other improvements) are you considering in the next 5 years? If so, what type?

**12.** Are you considering other projects like this in the near future?

**13.** How do you decide the order of importance?

**14.** What budget range of payment would you comfortable with? Use 3 ranges of payments such as: ($200-$300) or ($300-$400) or ($400 and up).

**15.** Is there anyone else you rely on to make a decision like this?

**16.** Our customers say there are some very important things they need to know in order to make an educated decision on a project like this. What things are important to you?

Let them think for a few minutes; then, let them answer in their own words. Write their words down and then lead them to answers that you already have on the bottom of your survey.

These are the ones we use in our industry which are key to making their purchase a solid investment as well as being the items that set us apart from the competition:

♦ Company
♦ Product
♦ Warranty
♦ Workmanship
♦ Return on Investment

**17.** Once you find someone who satisfies all things, that's when the shopping stops?

Don't be afraid to use this. It's quite interesting that most people will answer every question without hesitation and almost everyone says YES to the final question! This "yes" puts you in the position that if you can satisfy all of those things in your presentation that you will make a sale.

By using a written survey form, we're creating more needs for the product. By asking open-ended questions, listening to the answers and recording the answers on paper and encouraging them to elaborate on why they want (and need) this product we have tools that will help us close the sale.

Start painting the picture of how the new product will change their life: save time, more convenience, prestige, pride, save energy, expands the home, etc.

Don't let negative answers to any of the survey questions effect your presentation. You are only collecting information here, not selling, so don't worry about excuses or objections, and don't change or stop your presentation because of something they say that you perceive as something that may kill the sale.

If you find your prospect trying to stop you during the survey to move forward; to see the product or get a price, don't get concerned. You may be moving along too slowly (so pick up the pace) or you may be making them defensive with what sounds to them like a series of personal questions. By reading the customer, you can make the choice here to move ahead or stay on track and finish the survey.

Remember, you are the professional, and based on the answers, you're going to recommend your practical solutions.

# Step 5

## Company Story

# Step 5: Company Story

*"Let me tell you a little about my company."* You must point out the reasons that others have chosen your company over the competition and why they never regret it.

You'll find that your customers that have decided to do business with you in the past are always happy to tell you what impressed them or what they thought was special about doing business with you.

These customers will also be happy to write a letter or do a quick video testimonial saying how satisfied they are, if you ask them. Testimonials sell, so getting them for your marketing material is important!

When you survey your previous customers, you may be surprised to know that price is rarely the most important deciding factor.

The following are some deciding factors we use in our presentation. We call them "**company pledges**":

- ♦ **QUALITY CONTROL**
- ♦ **FIRST QUALITY MATERIALS**
- ♦ **CERTIFIED MASTER CRAFTSMEN**
- ♦ **WORKMAN'S COMPENSATION**
- ♦ **LIABILITY INSURANCE**

- ◆ **RELEASE OF LEINS**
- ◆ **NO HIDDEN CHARGES**
- ◆ **COURTEOUS ESTIMATES**
- ◆ **INSPECTION UPON COMPLETION**
- ◆ **BANK RATE FINANCING**

Example: *"With ABC Company, Quality Control starts with your first contact: Julie, who answered the phone when you called, and Pete, who set the appointment and my visit today.*

*Quality control continues all the way through our process with the design, selection and ordering of the products and the scheduling of the project; as well as service after the sale."*

Each of these pledges is a feature about your company. These are the features that set you apart from your competition. You must present an advantage plus the benefit for each. This answers the prospects questions such as: "How is this company different?" and "What's in it for me?"

By presenting this information, you are giving the prospect the information required to make them feel comfortable about moving forward *and* instilling a 'sliver of doubt' about the competition's abilities.

The fact is, "If they (the competition) didn't mention it, they probably don't have it."

Always use 'Tie Downs'- "*Is _____ important to you?*" "*Does ABC sound like the kind of company you would feel comfortable doing business with?*"

By obtaining commitments (tie downs) along the way you're eliminating your competition and 'being selected' as the company your prospect wants to do business with.

During the close, your tie-downs allow you to quote their words back to them that they are committed to your company, products, services and you.

After you tell your story (peppered with your company pledges), it is the time to move onto the "Product" step of your presentation...

"*I know we have taken several minutes reviewing our pledges. HAVE YOU LEARNED SOME THINGS THAT MAY HELP YOU?*"

# Step 6
## Setting the Stage

# Step 6: Setting the Stage

This is the time to put the customer at ease and set the stage for the close. Always give the setting the stage story **BEFORE** going into the product demonstration.

After you "tie down" your pledges...hesitate and then say, *"Remember that I told you before that we service such a large territory? If you noticed I couldn't get out here really fast. I usually don't know day to day where I will be. It might be in the east area one day and in the west on the next. I keep a really busy schedule and do lots of traveling."* (NOTE: this is an example.)

*"I'm the (Designer, Representative, etc.) for the company. I take care of the issues between our customers, office and installation and overall business development. We've had an overwhelming response to some of the advertising that we've been doing. Sometimes we don't always have enough representatives to cover all of the inquiries and sometimes our customers have to wait too long for us to visit."*

Strong validation of your position is a requirement. If your prospect sees you as a leader in your company or the person in charge of the negotiation with them, they are likely to be more honest about what is REALLY going on in their mind and give you the real objection like "price sounds too high," rather than an excuse like "we are getting other estimates." This allows you to deal with the objection early and directly.

You are setting the stage for the close, knowing they are likely to give you an excuse that may require you to come back to see them at a later date. In your close, you can refer to what you've said here as your reason to give them an incentive to move forward.

You'll learn more about this in the "close." Make sure they have your business card at this point.

# Step 7

## Product

## Demonstration

# Step 7: Product Demo

**Know your products and services and know your competitor's products.** If you have trouble explaining your products, the customer will dismiss you quickly. If you are not an expert they'll find someone who is. The bottom line on product is: If you don't know your product and your competitor's products you'll be forced to sell based on price alone.

**The formula for a masterful presentation:**

**Differentiate** - There are many things that make you and your company special and different from your competitors: personalized service, certifications, special products or systems and YOU. Highlight those things! If your competitor didn't mention it, they probably don't have it! By pointing that out you'll establish a 'sliver of doubt' about your competitors.

**WIIFM (What's in it for me) feature,**

**advantages + benefit** - Many "salespeople' present features and forget to describe the advantage and benefit of the features. You must put yourself in your prospect's shoes and say: "What's in it for me?"

**Hold their attention-ask questions** - The best way to keep someone's attention is to ask questions and keep him or her involved. Throughout your presentation use 'tie-downs' such as *"Hearing that (what I've just told you), doesn't my company sound like the type of company that if and when you do this, you would feel comfortable doing business with?"*

**Entertain** - Most people that choose sales as a profession have wit and are entertaining to communicate with. Relax, enjoy yourself and don't be afraid to show them your personality!

**Make it fun** - Sales can be a really fun career. As you've been instructed, your presentation should be scripted. Even if you use the same silly joke in your presentation, it will be their first time hearing it!

**Keep them involved, mentally and physically** - If you have samples, photos, data or examples to show them, put it in their hands. Let them see and feel the product. Your prospect is always willing to help you with measuring or paperwork like a credit application. If you keep them involved, you'll keep their attention, and if they are helping you with pricing, etc. they'll believe your figures.

**Ask open-ended questions; listen completely to the answers** - Your questions should be memorized, such as in the Entry and Warm-Up: *"How long have you lived here? Where are you originally from?*

*How do you like the area? What type of work do you do?"*

Remember; always ask your question to both if there are two parties. The one you leave out may kill your sale.

**Design solutions** - Your level of confidence will play a major role in closing each sale. If you are not convinced in the value of your proposal or if you are confused, your customers will know it. If you are confident that you have designed solutions accurately, your customers will have confidence in you.

## Recap & Restate Urgency

This is the time to present the full project description, the complete offer and have the customers agree that the description is exactly that they want. If possible this full description should be in writing on a proposal or sales agreement. *"The project includes..."* and describe it as completely as possible.

Try to leave no questions regarding the project/offer: "The type of company you said you want, the product, skilled workers and superior warranty."

While calculating the price you may want your customer to help so the customers trust your figures.

# Step 8

## Pricing

# Step 8: Pricing

### Prewriting the Agreement

As your prospect makes his selections, pre-write the agreement, if your paperwork is simple enough to make this possible. Write the details and selections into your order form. Most people are not likely to get defensive about you "selling" them if they see the agreement before you've done the pricing.

**Note:** Interestingly enough, very few prospects will ever question why you're filling out the paperwork. If they do, simply state: *"I'm just writing down what we're discussing."* By prewriting the agreement, frequently it will allow you to obtain an impulsive commitment once the price is presented. This close is called "assuming the order."

If you have the details of the project on an agreement, once you've calculated the price, you can read the agreement (complete description of the offer), present the price, then ask a simple question like, *"How do you spell your last name?" "Do you use a middle initial?"* or *"What is your street number here?"*

You appear to be formalizing the paperwork, so if they have an objection they may stop you here. If not, after reading the full description and specifications and presenting the price, just say: *"All I need is your*

*OK right here,"* while handing them the pen and
pointing to the place to OK the agreement.

Remember, you have made a complete presentation,
made friends, established trust, eliminated the competition and moving forward to your prospect may
seem perfectly natural. Although you need more than
"just" an OK on the agreement to get things moving,
you should approach the commitments in stages (one
by one) to make it sound natural and simple to move
forward.

### Presenting the Price

Before presenting the price you must present the full
description of the project, (everything that is included
in the offer). You must also present the available
terms and payment options. Your offer must be crystal clear so that once the price is in front of them
there are no product questions like: "Is this or that
included?" After reviewing the full scope of the project
it is time to quote the price.

### Pricing and Payment Quote

Design a simple pricing and payment quote on a
spreadsheet like the following. This can easily be
done in Excel and be protected so that the formulas
don't accidentally get changed. The items entered to
obtain the calculations are the total investment and
the custom payment term. This sheet has payments

calculated without using the deposit, which would allow you then to negotiate the deposit out of the transaction during the close.

**Pricing Payment Quote**
National Average          $ 30,720.00
Total Investment          $ 25,600.00
**Option A:** 50% + 50%
$ 12,800.00
$ 12,800.00
**Option B:** 33% + 33% + 33%
$ 8,524.80
$ 8,524.80
$ 8,524.80
**Option C:** Custom Pay Plan
Deposit 10% $ 2,560.00
60 Months $ 512.00
120 Months $ 298.67
180 Months $ 227.56
240 Months $ 192.00

**Always Present the Price with Confidence, and In This Way:**
Present a "national average" pricing - add 20% to your quote. Think about it, you can always find a competitor with a price 20% higher.

Present the national average as a whole number in "Thousands" such as "*Thirty thousand, seven hundred twenty dollars."* Then present your price this way: *"Your total investment on the complete project right now is only...twenty five, six."* ($25,600).

The reason for presenting the numbers this way is that leaving out the "thousands" and "dollars" makes their total investment number sound smaller.

Say: *"There are basically three ways you can take care of this: Option A: 50% with the order and 50% on completion. Option B: 1/3 with the order, 1/3 at the start and the final 1/3 on completion or the Custom Pay Plan: with only a 10% deposit and a payment as low as only ($192) 'One hundred ninety two per month."*

Quote your lowest available payment. Silence is golden at this point. Once the price and payment options are in front of them it is extremely important to remain completely silent. The masters of closing sales say: **"He who speaks first loses!"**

### Be Patient

The silence may seem to go on forever; five minutes to you may seem like forever because you are waiting for what happens next. Realize though, how much information the prospect has in front of him to absorb.

You may have been there for two hours and have presented a tremendous amount of information. The price is what they've been waiting for but they have much more than just the price in front of them under consideration.

At this point, you are saying nothing, and they will speak first. What are they likely to say? The exciting thing is that as an educated sales professional, you already know what they are likely to say!

You may get a surprise. If one party says: *"Wow, that's a lot of money!"* Wait a few seconds to respond, because the other party may say: *"That's half of what I thought it would be!"*

This is why you always want to be aware that if you are dealing with two or more interested parties, you're likely to have more than one opinion. One party can cancel out another party's objection.

One party may say: *"Wow!"* and you may assume they say that because the price is too high. Always ask, *"Why or what do you mean by 'Wow!'?"*

They may have said *"Wow!"* because the price is less than they thought it would be! If this is the situation you are faced with, it would be really easy to move forward with the paperwork and wrap up the sale without even asking for the order.

You're not really selling yet. You've given them lots of information. They may ask, *"How long is this price good for?"* or *"Is this your best price?"* These questions are exciting to hear because these are buying questions.

**"How long is this price good for?"**
Automatically say: *"This quote is good for 30 days,"* because you're not really selling yet. You've given them a quote with no discounts that's good for 30 days. You're sitting in the driver's seat because they are not being pushed into a decision yet.

**"Is this your best price?"**
Ask: *"How soon do you plan to move forward?"* If your industry or your company has periodic sales or offers discounts, the answer will open the door to refer to the advertisement...or source of inquiry, offer or discount (confirm where they said they heard about you).

# Step 9

## Closing

# Step 9: Closing

When the price is out, be prepared to hear objections. Understand first, that objections are a sign of interest and that the first objection you hear is usually not the real objection. The "rule of sixes" in sales says that the first five objections are excuses and not the prospect's real reasons not to buy.

Once the price is out, the prospect will likely say something like, *"Well, thanks for your time, we've got your card, we're going to think about it, talk about it, sleep on it, get other prices, go to our bank,"* etc.

Unfortunately, many salespeople accept what the prospect has said as the prospect's objection and pack up and leave. I sometimes say, on every appointment someone is sold. Either the prospect buys the product or the salesperson buys an objection.

You must always listen completely to the objection, then wait a few seconds and ask why they say what they've said.

If you are unable to get what sounds like a real answer, casually ask, *"If we did get together in the next 30 days, which payment option would you be most comfortable with...A, B or C?"*

When you are closing, be aware of your body language. You don't want your customer to get defensive. When closing sales and overcoming objections, relax, lean back as though you are just having a friendly conversation.

### Closing the Sale

"What are you using for your close?" "What do you say that is closing sales for you?" These are the questions most asked when experienced salespeople get together.

Usually, they'll tell each other what they say in the "closing" step of their presentation. The fact is, if everything was done properly throughout the presentation up to the point of "closing," most sales will automatically close and many more sales will consistently be made.

If sales are not consistently being made, more discipline or training may be required. What it comes down to is that when you are properly using a systematic presentation, sales will close automatically, because you have made friends, established trust, shown the value of your company, product and personnel, eliminated the competition and created urgency.

## "Much Is Lost By Not Asking"

Asking for the order is "the key" to successful selling. Remember as a child asking a parent for something and they said "no"? Then you asked the same question again and again and finally they said "OK"?

Sometimes "no" is an automated response and your prospect has no real reasoning behind it. This is why you must ask "Why?" frequently. You must do it in a specific way so the prospect doesn't see it as pressure or a confrontation.

In order to close without pressure, you must possess a structured, word-for-word, memorized close that is clear and simple, and that everyone is likely to understand. If the prospect is confused about your offer during your close, the sale will be lost.

The close must feel comfortable to you so that you will continue using it. But remember, you'll have to get outside your usual comfort zone to close sales.

Use your close every time, even when faced with an objection that you can't seem to overcome and that you totally believe to be true and real. Make the close an automatic component of your sales presentation; make it yours and practice, practice, practice.

## One Chance!

In most direct selling businesses, you must realize that the only chance we will ever have to close the sale is the first time we have given the customer a complete demonstration. They will never be more excited about your company, your product, your offer, or you than while you are sitting in front of them.

In order to make a complete presentation, we must have all decision-makers present and be able to give a full, controlled presentation. Flexibility may be needed as far as the order of presentation is concerned, but the complete presentation must be given and a "complete" presentation includes the close.

Many salespeople are really shy when it comes to closing the sale, hence the joke, "Timid salespeople have skinny children." Many times salespeople just don't know how to close, have never been taught or just feel awkward with the close that they've learned, so they simply don't use it. What I hope to accomplish is to give you a close that you can be comfortable with and consistently works.

Once the prospect has the information, they will usually say something like, *"Well, thanks for spending the time with us and giving us this information and price. We've got your card, we'll give you a call when we decide."*

The inexperienced salesperson says, "OK, well, call me when you're ready," or "When can I call you?" then leaves empty handed!

## Discounting

Discounts, if presented properly, work well for closing sales. Remember though, most purchases are not made because of discounts or a low or lowest price. If you are selling low prices or big discounts, I recommend that you stop! Low price may seem to be a path of least resistance but low price is not the key to making sales.

If your industry permits discounting price or offering an incentive to obtain an order, you can get the objections funneled down to price quite easily, then use a price discount or incentive as the basis for creating urgency and moving forward while you are there.

When you or your company are advertising discounts, quote the retail (full value price) then wait for the customer to ask for the discount or sale price. This indicates a high level of interest.

Hold back on the advertised discount for those who want to move forward. If your company offers or advertises discounts, be sure to always offer them and don't ever "over" discount the price. If a discount is currently advertised you must offer it. The reason for not offering the advertised discount initially is that some prospects may not want to move forward right away and may miss out on the savings. If the advertisement has a limit such as $500 or $1,000 only use that number as the discount and no higher.

Large discounts do not close sales and may cost you your credibility. Show the full dollar number of the discount and present it in a way that creates urgency: *"Right now I can save you one-thousand, five hundred dollars on this project, which brings your total investment down to only eighteen, eight oh four."*

The words "right now" are used specifically to create urgency. Do not give the time line on the discount, wait for them to ask. By asking they are showing a high level of interest. The word "only" is to let them believe that you perceive this as a low price (by saying it this way the price may sound low to them).

With or without discounts you must show the value, sell the value and present your price with confidence.

**Timing for Closing the Sale**
After receiving a roadblock objection, like *"We have to think about it,"* or *"We have to talk about this,"* you cannot just ignore this objection and 'move on' to another close. You must 'dig in' and try to overcome the objections. When presented with an objection

(excuse), hesitate then ask: *"Why?"* or *"Why do you say that?"*

Be sure that both or all the parties agree on what the objection is. Say to the silent party: *"Is that how you feel, too?"* or *"What do you think?"*

When you ask, "Why?" the customer will usually say: *"Because that's the way we do things, it's just the way we do business, it's just our policy to think or talk things over before we make a decision."*

Then say, *"Just to add some clarity to my thinking, what is the reason that you have adopted that decision-making policy?"* In many cases this will uncover the REAL objection and allow you to move forward toward the close.

After doing what you can with the objections (excuses), your prospect is going to get to the point where they have given you a "final" objection and are trying to say goodbye by saying something like, *"Well, thanks for everything, we'll get back to you."*

Remember though, this is all very friendly and conversational, no pressure, no confrontation. If you do all of your closing properly, your customer is likely to thank you for not pressuring them.

Sales is a conveyance of ideas and they are making their own decision based on the information that you are presenting.

### Close

After the price has been presented, they may say, *"Sounds great, let's do it!"* and that's nice when they do, but be prepared for a general response like, *"That sounds OK, thanks for the estimate."*

Usually they will not make a commitment here, but just be patient and listen. If they give you an objection, don't be alarmed. If they remain quiet simply ask, *"How does that sound?"*

The close is where objections (excuses) must be addressed and overcome in an attempt get to the real objection. You must assume that you are only dealing with excuses at this juncture. Think of the national average pricing as "price conditioning." Your quoted price may close the sale, but you are a professional, you're holding the cards, so you have other plans if it doesn't. After the price has been presented it is time to "sell."

Planning for objections prepares you for another step in the process of closing sales. Remember, after the price is out you are going to hear some untruths.

They don't want to hurt your feelings, or they want to get other prices, etc. so don't believe everything you hear.

**No Pressure**

After they have responded to the price and given you some feedback or objections, say, *"This quote is good for 30 days."* This statement takes the pressure off.

Ask, *"If and when you do move forward on the project, how would you be handling it, cash, credit card or financing?"*

They should not be feeling any pressure at this point, so they're likely to give you some honest feedback.

Explain the terms again:
*"Option A: 50% with the order, 50% on completion or Option B: 1/3, 1/3, 1/3 or the custom payment plan."*

Review the offer and relax as if you're done, then start packing some things up as if you're getting ready to leave. Casually say, *"I get the feeling that you folks really like what you have seen here today and that you are going to do this."*

Understand that they will usually say, *"Yeah, I think we are, but..."* You'll hear one of five objections (the big five "excuses"):

1. Think about it,
2. Too much money,
3. Shop around,
4. Talk to someone else
5. We never do business on the first day (or first visit with a salesperson).

Remember that these are usually just excuses. What you are really trying to do here is find the real objection. Basically the excuse here is a "not making a decision now" or a time stall.

At this point, ask, *"How long do you think that will take? When would you want me to get back to you on this?"* They may say *"two weeks or four weeks or not until spring."* Whatever the answer is, always respond with, *"That soon?"*

If they start going back and forth (playing verbal ping pong), *"What do you think? Well, what do you think?"* say, *"Time out! This is how we do it..."* (my wife and I, or most of my customers) *"If John said he really likes this and he wants to move forward, would you object, Mary? So John, if Mary said she likes it and wants to do it, would you object?"*

Then continue, *"Well let me ask you this, other than the money would there be any reason that we couldn't move forward?"*

Use the first visit offer: "Tomorrow is going to be no different."

## The "Final" Objection

Once you receive an objection that appears to be the "final" or "real" one, ask, *"Other than that, (the objection) would you be moving forward on the project?"*

Once you've said this, the objection is likely to change...eventually it may come down to price.

## Evaluation: One to Four Stars

You must get your prospect to give you an honest evaluation of your presentation. Design a form and call it "one to four stars."

Introduce it as if you've just remembered that you must do your "quality control survey." *"By the way, before I leave, I'd like to ask you (or say, my company requires me to ask you) a few questions for our quality control."*

When you gave your pledges you'll have mentioned "Quality Control," so it won't come as a complete surprise that you're presenting this. Ask them to be completely honest and assure them that they won't hurt your feelings.

## Company Name
## Company Logo

### ONE TO FOUR STARS

| | 1 Star | 2 Stars | 3 Stars | 4 Stars |
|---|---|---|---|---|
| Company: | | | | |
| Product: | | | | |
| Design: | | | | |
| Representative: | | | | |
| Price: | | | | |

Customer: _____     Date: _____

The purpose of the "one to four stars" is to confirm that your prospect(s) agree that they like the company, design, product and you. You'll almost always get four stars on all of these.

This narrows the objection down to only price and sets you up with the opportunity to deal with the issue of price.

You want to confirm and reassure the value, downscale the project to their affordability, lower the payment (with a longer term), eliminate or lower the deposit, etc. Many times you'll only receive 2 stars on the price, which is exciting because the door has just re-opened to make a sale.

**NOTE:** See the simple template I use on the page on your left. You can download this at www.sellsellsellbook.com, as well for your convenience.

### "Keep Smiling and Keep Asking"

Your prospect knows that you are there to make a sale. It's a good idea to ask for permission to close during your 'company story' portion of the presentation by saying, "*You wouldn't get upset if I asked for your business at least once while I'm here, would you?*"

During the close make this statement: *"I know you really like what I've shown you here today and I really would love to earn your business while I'm here."*

### Initial Visit Close

This close does not have to be a money drop, but some type of incentive for someone who is willing to move forward. Use this only if your company or your industry allows incentives or discounts for a first visit order.

As if it just came to mind say, *"I don't offer this to everyone, but I can see how serious you folks are about having this done."* (Pause)

Most will not respond to this, they usually just remain quiet. If you are presenting to more than one party, not answering this statement lets both parties believe that the other is very interested. No one ever says, *"I'm not that interested."*

*"The reason I don't offer this to everyone is because it makes me a little uncomfortable and kind of puts you on the spot."*...An honest statement, huh?

Then say, *"Let me tell you how it works. Some folks we see are ready to make their decision on the first visit. Other people need more time. Sometimes requiring a second, third or even a fourth visit and that's quite all right. But, you know the people we visit once or the people we visit several times all pay the same amount even though we have a lot more invested in gas, time and expenses in sending a representative out.*

*The largest expense though, is that representative is not available for visiting other interested people. So what my company has implemented is a way to pass on the savings of seeing someone only once; it's like profit sharing."*

Then continue, *"So let me ask you a question..."* Then hesitate. This statement gets their full attention for your offer.

*"If there were a way that that I could make a special offer on the project...something really nice...if I could do that for you and you liked that offer would there be any reason that we couldn't move forward while I'm here?"* This narrows the objection down to price or affordability and puts you in a position to deal with only one objection.

**Note:** Lowering price is not the point here. Price and value must match your customer's values and affordability. You are now in a position to design what you are selling to meet their affordability. Most importantly, though, you are getting honest feedback from your soon-to-be new customer.

**Important:** To successfully accomplish this close, it must be memorized and presented word for word.

Wait for a commitment or rejection. You hope they say, "Depends on how much." Then you can move forward with your offer and a close. If they say, "*No, we can't make a commitment,*" then don't give the incentive or discount and ask, "*Why?*"

**Note:** You must have a commitment before presenting the offer, otherwise you are just throwing something else in on the quote and they'll likely ask, "*How long is that price good for?*" or say, "*Well we'll give you a call when we decide.*"

### Closing Statements

You've heard lots of excuses and objections and you sense your customer is on the fence. It usually only takes a little nudge to get them to move forward.

Remember, you have made friends with them at this point; you know that they want or need the product and you can get away with a little "encouragement."

Try one of these questions or statements. They REALLY work!

**1.** "*Mary, would you be upset if John went ahead and let me put you folks on the schedule?*"

**2.** "*She (or he) really wants the project; she's already* *told us that. What d'ya say, let's just go ahead and do it!"*

**3.** *"Why don't you folks have a little confidence in me and let me go ahead and do this project for you?"*

**4.** *"C'mon, let's just go ahead and put this on the schedule!"*

**5.** *"Let me ask you this..."* (This is an attention getter.) *"What if I could...do something really special for you...give you an additional incentive...do the project sooner...do the project for less...make a telephone call to help you out with:* (price or whatever the objection might be)*...throw in a...move you up on the schedule, etc. ...If I could do that for you, would you let me put you on the schedule while I'm here?"* (This last part must be included for urgency.)

**6.** Here's a funny one; I've never actually used it but saw it used once (we didn't make the sale, by the way!) *"Isn't true that when you first met your wife, you loved her so much you would have bought two of these? Well, don't you love her half as much now?"*

**Selling Financing**

**Note:** Many companies do not have payment options for their potential customers. This is easy to resolve because all banks want your customers to borrow money from them.

Simply set up a customer referral program with the manager a local bank.

Show the initial investment and say: *"If we got to-gether in the next 30 days, would you be comfortable with this as an initial investment?"*

Use a "choice close" on the financing on every cus-tomer. Use 5, 7, and 10-year terms or 5, 10, 15 and 20 depending on the size of the investment. The cus-tomer may ask if you have 100% financing, which could be your closing tool: **"What if I could, would you...?"**

Use the highest interest rate that they might experi-ence for payment quotes. When their payment comes in lower, they'll have a pleasant surprise. Try not to quote what the actual interest rate is. You may nudge them towards the longest payment term to make them more comfortable about moving forward.

Customer says: "What's your rate?"
**Answer:** *"I can't answer that. Not to be evasive, but I would have to know your credit rating. We use this payment chart which reflects the highest rate so I could probably save you some on the payment."*
Customer says: "We are going to get our own financ-ing from our bank or credit union."
**Answer:** *"Why don't we do this? I'll get this approved through my source, so we can go ahead and put your project on the schedule and honor the savings. If you want to check your own bank, we could compare the*

*rates we come up with. You are not obligated to the
financing until the work is done. Because of the excep-
tionally high resale value of these products, you would
actually add much of the value of the project to the
asking price of your home."*

If they say they don't want to commit until the financing has been approved (be careful, this may be
an excuse), say *"We all know the bank has someone
just waiting for you folks to walk through the door to
give them some money. You wouldn't be obligated if
you couldn't get the money anyway,* (keep moving) *but
that's not a problem, let's get this started."* Pull out a
credit application and start filling it out (assuming
the sale).

### Down Payment (Initial Investment) Close

During the presentation they may have said, "I don't
know how I/we would pay for something like this,"
and in order to diffuse the objection you may have
made the comment that "You don't have to pay for it
until it is completed."

Don't bring the subject of the down payment up at
any time during the presentation; the customer may
view it as negative. If they bring down payment
(initial investment) up, this is another sign of a high
level of interest. The reality is, the larger the deposit
you receive, the lower the chance of cancellation.

Successful salespeople will work as hard for a solid deposit as they will to make the sale itself. Use this statement: *"Company policy is one third, but whatever you can give me today."*

The objective is to get them to tell you what is affordable for them to give you with the order. Many cash buyers will want to impress you that they can actually give you a check for that amount.

### Positive Language
We always talk differently behind closed doors than we do in front of a customer. Your sales or "industry" terms will not sound the same to your prospect or customer as they do to you and your peers.

It is extremely important to speak in terms that will make the prospect feel that he is not dealing with a "slick" salesperson. Look at the table on the next page to help you adjust your language...

**Note:** Check out the chart on the next page and read it several times to condition yourself to use this positive language.

### Keys to a Successful Close
• Establish your position: "I'm a really busy person; it'll be difficult to come back again later."
• Pre-write the agreement (assume the sale).

| Negative | Positive |
|---|---|
| Contract | Agreement or Paperwork |
| Deal | Value or Opportunity |
| Price | Your Investment |
| Down Payment | Your Initial Investment |
| Buy | Own or Acquire |
| Monthly Payment | Monthly Investment |
| Sign | Approve, Authorize or O.K. |
| Appointment | Visit |
| Commitment | Yea or Nay or OK |
| Lead | Customer, Meeting or Appointment |
| Problem | Challenge or Hurdle |

• Present the price and payment options clearly and with confidence.

• When the price is out, remain silent; he who speaks first loses.

• Anticipate excuses and objections (you're holding aces, because you know how to deal with them).

• IROC (Isolate, Restate, Overcome, Close)

**When Customers Say "No";**
**Sales Professionals Understand...**

**1.** Most customers give excuses instead of real reasons not to buy. The 'rule of sixes' says you will hear five excuses on the average before hearing the real objection.

**2.** Do not risk your sale on an excuse. The real objection is behind those excuses.

**3.** Give empathy to open the customer's mind. Examples: *"I understand," "I hear what you are saying,"* or *"I'm just like you, I usually feel that way too."*

**4.** The first time you hear a particular objection, it may be handled by just ignoring the objection. You didn't hear it, you don't respond and you move forward in an attempt to close the sale.

**5.** After hearing an objection that must be addressed, you must clarify it and make sure you understand it.

**6.** I.R.O.C. (Isolate, Rephrase, Overcome, Close)

• **Isolate**: Isolate the objection that you've been presented with as the objection that is preventing them from moving forward. *"Other than that (objection),*

*then could we go ahead and put you on the schedule?"*
• **Rephrase**: *"So what you're saying is, you can't move forward until: you get other estimates, financing is secured, etc."*
• **Overcome**: *"We've been in business for X years and wouldn't have been in business that long if our prices were high, don't you agree?" or "We have several financing sources, I'm sure I can obtain the financing for you at an acceptable rate."*
• **Close**: *"Let me ask you this...What if I could save you some money, get you the financing for less; would you let me go ahead and put you on the schedule?"*

***"What if I could...would you..." is THE key closing question and can be used on almost any objection such as price, payment, delivery date, shopping around, or talking to friends or family. This is the opening for the special offer (everyone wants a special!)

**7.** Ask lots of questions; the more information you get, the stronger you can reply.
• Investigate.
• Repeat the objection in your own words to see if you really understand it.
• Close doors.
• Resist the urge to sell until you are sure that you understand the objection.
• Listen to the customer. Understand that the object-

tion you are hearing is most likely not the real objection.

**8.** Usually, the first objection will be general in nature: *"We want to talk or think about it before we make a decision."* The automatic answer should be: *"Why?"* Or *"Why do you say that?"*

**9.** Qualify the objection as the reason holding them back from going ahead with the project. *"If we could put that (the objection) aside, otherwise you would be going ahead with the project?"*

**10.** If they say no to the qualifying question, then what you're hearing is an excuse and is not the objection. You must then ask for the real reason that is holding them back. Say, *"Just to clarify my thinking, could you explain..."*

**11.** If they say yes, then you have their commitment. They will buy if you answer their objection.

**12.** Once you feel prepared to answer their objections effectively, sell!

**13.** State your points strongly and clearly as facts. Confidence is really important here. Make at least three or four statements that are direct answers to their objections.

**14.** To allow them to change their mind from saying "no" without loss of face, state a logical advantage and emotional value that they will receive for going ahead. *"I understand what you're saying* (your objection), *but unfortunately this may not be available at a later date and we all know how much you will both* *enjoy the product once it's done!"*

**15.** Restate their total dollar savings for going ahead as opposed to waiting.

**16.** Close at least five times to ensure that you have given them the opportunity to buy.

**A Sales Professional Will Always...**
• Do a quality presentation with all the parts and pieces in place.
• Overcome objections before they come up.
• Eliminate the competition:
• No other company has what you have to offer, and they don't have YOU.
• Establish that sliver of doubt about your competitor's ability to provide what you can.
• Build urgency early in the presentation and maintain it throughout the entire presentation.
• Use the time line close and do it very well, (the "sale," schedule, material prices, etc.)
• Use tie-downs throughout your presentation: "Is this the (type of product, etc.) you had in mind?" Are we the type of company you would want working on your home?"
• Insist that this is the right decision for them and the right time to move forward. (Close them.)
• Realize that the first visit is the time to close the sale because their interest will never be higher than while you are there.

## A Real Professional Will...

♦ Be confident when presenting price.

♦ Always believe he can close.

♦ Never risk the sale on an excuse.

♦ Understand that objections are a sign of interest.

# Step 10

## Post-Close

# Step 10: Post-Close

Many sales are lost when the salesperson makes a sale and runs out the door. Once the paperwork is done and all the details have been covered, go back to the same conversations that you had during the warm up step of the presentation.

Reassure your customer that they have made a friend and do a complete review of what happens next to eliminate any surprises or misunderstandings.

Finally, find out whom they know that might also be interested in your services. Many companies offer referral fees, but get your customers to do it for *you*.

Remember, you all have made new friends and will look forward to helping each other out.

When you are sure they are comfortable with everything, say again, *"Thanks again for having confidence in me and my company. We'll do a wonderful job for you!"*

When exiting, always say, *"I had a great time here today and feel more like I was on a social visit than a sales call!"*

# Closing Summary

I typically teach the basics of the selling process, and then add to it. Becoming successful in sales requires practice and discipline. Sometimes you must get outside your normal comfort zone to close sales. There is no exact science to sales. The following are more tips to the close, but remember; the key ingredients are you, your desire, your attitude and your enthusiasm!

**NOTE**: If you enjoyed this book and want hands-on, face-to-face, in-the-trenches training to help you ingrain these skills and methods into your brain, visit www.sellsellsellbook.com for details on my upcoming **Sell! Sell! Sell! Make More Money Seminars**.

**Eliminate the Competition**. Odds are you know more about your competition than your customer does. You have many points to sell about yourself, your company, your products, and your dedicated staff that will follow through and support your new customers. During your presentation you will point these things out while leaving a sliver of doubt in your prospect's mind about your competition.

**Ignoring Objections**: It is polite to listen and acknowledge what people are saying. An effective strategy, though, is to ignore the objection. At the beginning of my selling career, I had a difficult time grasping that concept. I told one of my first trainers about the objections (which later became excuses) that I was hearing. I can still hear him saying, "You didn't hear that...you didn't hear that...you didn't hear that" until I finally caught on.

You don't have to hear everything that is said. You didn't hear it, didn't acknowledge it, didn't have to deal with it and it magically disappeared!

**Close in a friendly, conversational manner**. If you have made a complete presentation and answered your customer's questions and concerns, you will not have to harass them into signing. You have the best products and services available anywhere for the majority of customers, and you are responsible for telling your customers about your program.

Beating up a customer to get a signature usually results in a cancellation. You can't read minds. Close each and every time, even if you feel there is nothing there. There are many surprises. Much is lost by not asking!

**Fill out all sales paperwork completely and accurately**. Get all necessary customer information while you are on the appointment. Having to call back or return to the customer is tedious and may cause a cancellation. Write as neatly and legibly as possible. This will decrease the likelihood of errors and assist in getting your orders processed quickly.

Do a complete job the first time! It always pays off.

Finally, after the sale, **make sure that your customers are feeling comfortable with their decision**. Explain who will be following up, and when. Assure them that they have made the best possible choice. If you tell them that you will call them with additional information, make sure that you follow through.

Neglecting small items will cause concern over your ability to deliver on the rest of the job. After every visit, send a handwritten thank you card, sale or not.

## KEYS TO SUCCESS:
- Cover every appointment, and be on time
- Conduct a sincere and thorough warm up
- Conduct a casual but thorough survey
- Make a complete presentation every time
- Know your products and your competitor's products
- Price accurately, present every detail
- Close in a friendly and conversational manner
- Use automatic, scripted closing techniques
- Fill out paperwork accurately and completely
- Offer assurance after the sale

• Send thank you cards to everyone you visit...
sale or not

• Market your customers after the sale

Your objective is to do a complete presentation with all of the elements that encourage the customer to make the natural decision and feel that they have made the decision on their own.

You want them to say, "Yes! This is right for us, we both agree (right company, right product and right price), it's a great investment, it will increase the quality of our lives, we weren't pressured into it, and we definitely can afford it. We have done the right thing."

## No remorse = no cancellation.

From the start of the presentation you must antici-pate the objections that you are going to get and be ready to deal with them in a friendly, conversational manner.

As a professional salesperson and a new friend, they must feel that you are simply having a conversation and giving them honest opinions and advice.

You want to guide and encourage them to come to their own conclusion. You want them to feel as if you are a professional consultant and friend guiding them through this process to get what they want and need.

**Tips:**

• Always compliment them and make them feel special. You are making friends.

• Always maintain control of the presentation. Get all interested parties to the decision making area. If the customer has questions from page ten and you are on page one, tell him so.

• Choice close on all of the options as your presentation goes along. This means: *"Do you prefer option-A or option-B?"* And get both to respond.

• Never close during the presentation. This means saying, "You are going to really like my price, I'm going to make you a great deal," or "Are we going to get together on this today?"

• When presenting the price: *"The full value price on your complete project is twenty thousand-nine hundred dollars. That's your complete bottom line investment."*

• Anticipate the response, "That's twice what we thought it would be!"

• If the customer asks how long the price is good for, never say "today only" or "for the next five minutes." <u>The close is not a time for humor.</u>

• Choice close cash or credit. Then remain silent!

## Your assignments for success:

- ♦ Write out your complete presentation
- ♦ Rehearse it (until it is masterful)
- ♦ Record it on video
- ♦ Have the sales pros around you view it
- ♦ Memorize your close
- ♦ Practice, practice, practice!

# BONUS
# SECTION

# Sales Observations

**"We're getting other estimates"**
If you find yourself hearing the same objection over and over it's time to work on it during the presentation. Like most objections, "We're getting other estimates" can be overcome during your presentation. If the competition is effectively eliminated during a complete presentation each and every time, this objection may not come up at all.

Your objective is to get both customers to agree on everything; that you have the product, price and design that are right for them. If your prospects have participated in your presentation, mentally and physically, and understand the way your company does business and that they may be 'taking a chance' (sliver of doubt) in doing business with someone else (another company), and have agreed that it is not what they want, during the close, they may be too embarrassed to say, "We're getting other estimates."

**Note**: If you do a complete presentation and leave the door open to allow an objection to come up during the close, you'll be 'chasing' the objection in order to make the sale.

## The Assumptive Close

If the price is out and there is a level of interest but no commitment on the project, this may be the time to assume the sale. Pull out (or turn around) the agreement or proposal, start writing, and ask, "How do you spell that last name?" or "What is the address here?"

## The Confidence Close

This can be used when you have done a successful presentation and have built a friendship with the customer (you'll know if you have) but can't get a commitment. The question that is difficult for the customer to say no to is, *"Why don't you have a little confidence in me and let me do this project for you?"* Say this in a sincere way and it really works!

## The Handshake Close

*"Thanks for having the confidence in me and my company; I'll do you a beautiful job!"*

## Post-Close Referral Script

*"John and Mary, thank you for having the confidence in me and my company and choosing us to do this project for you. I told you about our interactive marketing program and how our customers send us customers. I would like you to get your address book and give me some names of people you know that I can contact.*

*I would like to send them some information. So many people know someone that might be interested that I find it's worth my time to do this."*

**Note**: Asking for referrals will prevent cancellations, as your customers would have to tell their friends why they cancelled.

## Responses to Objections

Remember, objections are a sign of interest and remember the 'rule of sixes'! It's likely that you are hearing 'excuses' and not real objections. Usually, you'll have to respond to several objections and ask lots of questions and maybe say something like: *"Just be honest with me, don't worry about my feelings."*

If they feel that the price is too high or they have another concern they may just be trying to say, "Goodbye" in a nice way by just giving you an 'excuse'.

Your responses to most excuses or objections should be rehearsed and perfected. Training through role-play can help accomplish this. Your responses should become automatic because you know that these objections are coming, especially once the price is out.

Don't 'jump' on the objection, hesitate for a few seconds before responding and make sure both parties agree to the objection that they are giving you before you respond to it. **Note**: A good way to learn how to respond is to practice using flash cards like you did in your early learning years. Remember flash cards? Your prospect says "this," you hesitate and say "that."

Select the responses that you are most comfortable with, practice and don't be afraid to go outside your comfort zone overcoming objections and Make More Money!

## "WE WANT TO THINK IT OVER. LEAVE YOUR CARD."

• *"I'm curious as to why you feel that way. Could you tell me?"*

• *"Some people do like to think about it, but just so that I am clear on this, is it the product you want to think about or the investment?"*

• *"I understand. What don't you feel comfortable with?"*

• *"Usually, that means there is something I haven't made clear. Could you share with me what it is?"*

• *"Terrific! Could you tell me what part of the things we spoke about that you want to go over in your mind?"* (Product, company or price.)

• *"There is no better time to think about the questions than when you have a "product" professional sitting right in front of you. Ask away!"*

• *"John and Mary, since I've been doing this for a long time, I understand, most people are not worried about making the decision, the issue is that they want to make the right decision. Is that how you feel?"*

• *"John and Mary, did something happen at one time or another to make you super-cautious about decisions?"*

• *"There's nothing wrong with that. Just remember though, each of us passed up some really good opportunities because we "paused" just a little too long. Why not look at the issues while I'm still here?"*

• *"Some people like to talk about things. How about if I let you two alone to "chat." I'll go outside and get some air and you can talk it over without me listening. Just let me know when you're ready."*

**There is no better way to practice these closes (*and others*) than in person with a coach and other sales experts.**

**For more information on Rick Edwards' Seminars and Programs, go here now: www.SellSellSellBook.com**

# "WE WANT TO CHECK YOUR REFERENCES."
### OR
# "WE WANT TO TALK TO SOME CUSTOMERS."
### OR
# "WE WANT TO SEE YOUR SHOWROOM OR A PROJECT YOU'VE DONE, FIRST."

• This can turn into a stall and prevent you from closing the sale. At first you may want to just ignore the 'excuse' and move on with the presentation or close.

Politely ignore this objection as if you'll get back to it. *"Oh yeah, I've got lots of references/customers."* Make them ask several times before you actually give them. (Sometimes they'll only ask once and forget about it.)

If you promise to get back to them with references, do it or they'll question your ability with follow through, which could mean you're likely to get a cancellation.

To answer a reference stall, *"Because so many of the homes we work on these days are owned by professional people, doctors and attorneys, they don't want their telephone numbers given out. I'll have to contact some customers and get back to you."*

**Note**: Don't let this stop you, move forward and close.

• If one of these 'stalls' turns into a real objection, say, *"When you check this out, I know you're going to love what you see and hear!*

*I'm also sure that you want to lock in the savings and get on the schedule to get this done. I'll go ahead and write the agreement contingent on you liking what you see* (or getting positive feedback)."

## "WE WANT TO CHECK OTHER PRICES. WE'LL CALL."

• *"Can you help me understand better? Is it that you want to shop around, or is it something else?"*

• *"I understand. Just so I can be clear as to what you mean, does that mean you don't like our price?"*

• *"Are you looking for something cheaper?"*

• *"I'm curious, what do you think you'll find in the market?"*

• *"Is it a lower price you want to shop for or better financing arrangements?"*

---

• *"A desire to check around indicates you are serious about having your project done. Could you share the type of product you want to check out?"*

Confirm the uniqueness of your product over the competition and set up for the first close. (Do the 'one to four stars' if you haven't already.)

• *"What you are telling me is you want to find the best product at the best price, right? If I could guarantee that you were getting the best product and the best price could I put you on the schedule?"*

• If they are "Waiting on the 'other' price": *"Professionals in this business can price the project while they are at the site; if they couldn't give you a quote while they were here, it's obvious that they aren't experienced or qualified."*

Confirm what other contractors might be involved, eliminate the competition, and close.

Eliminating One Competitor - If presented with this objection: *"We have one more estimate coming,"* ask: *"Would you mind telling me who it is?"*

You can eliminate one company with a single curious 'look' to which the customer will be very curious and pry, wanting to find out why you just did that. You'll have established that 'sliver of doubt'.

• Shopping for price indicates a desire to either spend less or to verify that a product is JUST RIGHT!
Ask: *"Is there something about our product you didn't like?"*

• *"You want to check other prices?"* (Silence)

## "WE'VE LIVED HERE A LONG TIME WITHOUT IT, WHY BUY NOW?"

• *"You've already told me you've both been thinking about this for a long time..."* (With excitement and enthusiasm) *"...Why don't we just go ahead and do it!"*

• *"Come on John, isn't it about time you made things easier on yourself and Mary? Just think about it..."*

• *"John and Mary, you've deprived yourself long enough. Do you know that some people use their time on pleasure instead of painting and cleaning? Why not you?"*

• *"John and Mary, just about half of our customers are folks like you on a fixed income. They want to save money and stop doing the hard work of cleaning and taking care of that area. I bet you feel the same, don't you?"*

• *"John and Mary, you have worked long and hard to buy and pay for this place, which is the biggest investment of your life. Not only would you be protecting your most important asset, you would get so many benefits. Let me repeat them."*

• *"Oh, c'mon, don't be so tough on yourself at this point in your life. It's time to take it easy. This product is exactly what you need!"*

• *"Because it's a no-lose investment. Your property goes up in value, and you live more comfortably while saving money."*

• *"Why not now? The "project" will never be less expensive and you can't afford to pass up these discounts. In time, it will pay for itself."*

• *"John and Mary, we must have been looking at a different project. Let me tell you what I saw."* (Repeat all the problems and solutions.)

## "WE HAVE A LOWER PRICE."

• *"I'm not surprised about that. Most companies know what their product is worth. What did you think about their quality?"*

• *"Honestly, I would prefer to apologize for price now than poor quality later. We only offer the best. You folks do see the value of what I've shown here, don't you?"*

Because they are being honest in telling you this, instead of giving you an excuse in an effort to save your feelings, it means that they want to find a way do business with you.

They want reassurance in your quality: company, products and people; that the quality of doing business with you is higher than the 'competition'.

## "WE'RE NOT READY RIGHT NOW!"

• *"Why do you say you are not ready?"*

• *"I understand. How soon would you be ready?"* No matter the length of time, respond with, *"THAT SOON?"*

- *"I understand. Is there a special reason you want to put off this decision? Would you share it with me?"*

- *"I understand you are not ready now, but let me ask you this...do you agree that sooner or later you are going to have to do something about having this project done?"*

- *"John and Mary, please take this the right way. You may not be ready, but your home sure is. You need this project."*

- *"If I could show you a program to do the project, get the savings, and delay any obligation to put out cash, would that have an appeal to you?"*

- *"Did something happen during a previous investment that makes you so cautious?"*

- *"Some people say that, but everybody can remember a time or two they missed an opportunity because they chose not to make a decision. Let me review the full impact of moving forward while I'm here."*

- *"Since you have indicated your need for and certainly like our product, what will have to change to get the project started?"*

• *"The savings to act now are large enough for us to "work this out." From a professional point of view, I'm a little confused as to what is stopping you."*

## "WE'RE NOT SURE WE CAN AFFORD IT RIGHT NOW."

### OR

## "THE PAYMENTS ARE TOO HIGH."

• *"Would you mind sharing with me why you feel that way?"*

• *"Is it the price, the payment, or the down payment that's bothering you?"*

• *"Other than that, is there anything else that would keep you from going ahead with this project?"*

• *"What payment would you like? What were you hoping it would be? Now, be reasonable."*

• *"Lots of folks feel that way at "first glance." Let me explain why the investment is not as much of a "cost" as you may think."*

• *"If I had been able to bring the investment in at a figure you were comfortable with, would you have gone ahead?"*

• *"Some people say that, but please remember that there is a difference between cost and investment."*

• *"Some people say that. Let me ask you how you felt about the product, other than the investment."*

• *"Some people say that, but a lot depends on what price you are willing to put on quality. These days, you only get what you pay for, isn't that so?"*

• *"John and Mary, is what you're saying to me is that you like the product, but it is simply too much money for your budget? What had you planned for? What were you hoping I would say?"*

## "WE DON'T MAKE A DECISION LIKE THIS ON THE SPOT."

• *"Why do you say that?"*

• *"I can understand that. Many people say that; it's the reason my company offers special incentives for people that do have the confidence to move forward. Let me explain how it works."*

• *"I can understand that, but remember, how many things have you put off until tomorrow and... tomorrow never came!"*

- *"I can appreciate how you feel. Many of my customers felt the same way. But as soon as I was clearly able to explain the "full" impact of the opportunity being presented, I found they wanted to take advantage of it. What haven't I explained clearly?"*

- *"I understand, but could you tell me, what will you know after you 'sleep on it'?"*

- *"That's understandable. Could I ask you what part of the decision you need more time to 'digest'?"*

- *"Many people are hesitant to decide right away. I'm going to ask you to use your intuition about our "talk" tonight. Why not just have confidence in my company and me and let me go ahead and do this project for you?"*

- *"I certainly understand. My wife and I like to speak in private about certain things, too. Let me step outside while the two of you talk it over."*

- *"My wife and I are similar to you. We like to mull over certain decisions, but we also have another rule. When a real opportunity presents itself, we can decide."*

- *"I understand what you're saying, but it certainly isn't a spur of the moment decision. You said earlier that you've been thinking about this for ___ number of years. Is there anything that I haven't explained clearly?"*

• *"John and Mary, you've already told me that you like the quality of the product and the integrity of the company. What don't you feel comfortable about?"*

• *"I understand. I have a feeling that the reason we can't get together is NOT that you can't make a decision... But that you want to be sure you're making the CORRECT decision. Is that correct?"*

• *"I understand. Please don't get upset over what I am about to say. John and Mary, if I ever saw a home that needed this product now, yours is it...and you agreed! I feel you really like my product as I showed it to you. Am I right about that? Then what is it? Is it the investment?"*

## "I WANT TO CHECK OUT YOUR COMPANY."

• *"You want to check out my company? I really owe you an apology. Since that is one of our strong points, I thought I covered that thoroughly. What is it that is still on your mind?"*

• *"Other than that, is there anything else that would keep you from going ahead?"*

• *"If that's all that is holding you back, we might as well put you on the schedule, because we are the best!"*

• *"What exactly do you want to check out? I told you about our memberships...etc."*

## "I WANT TO DISCUSS IT WITH MY RELATIVES-SON / DAUGHTER / PARENTS."

• *"You already know what they'll say, the same thing as you would say to them: "If you're comfortable with the offer, do what makes you happy."*

• *"What is it you wish to discuss?"*

• *"That's no problem. I have a feeling your son will think you have made a fine decision. He'd probably like...*
*a. That we have been in business since _____.*
*b. The "product" has such a strong warranty.*
*c. That you are saving ___ on the purchase.*
*d. The fact that you deserve the comfort, warmth and freedom from maintenance, etc."*

• *"My experience with sons/daughters/parents is that most family members are cut from the same mold. If you see value, they do too. But since it is YOU that will be getting the benefit, it really is YOUR decision, isn't it?"*

### Rules of the Road

This book is a path to guide you to success in your sales career. You must develop a complete systematic presentation and learn your products. You will also need to be familiar with other products used in the industry and your competition. Develop your people skills and learn closing techniques.

In order to more effectively coordinate your sales efforts and maximize every opportunity, here are some "RULES OF THE ROAD" to follow:

♦ Arrive meticulously on time.

♦ If all interested parties are not present, do a complete warm-up and build interest with the party that is there, then reset a time to see all/both parties.

♦ Do a complete presentation each and every time.

♦ Be cautious with your cellular phone. You don't want your customer insisting that you "take" that phone call that interrupts your close or, conversely, make him feel like you are ignoring him while you text or check your messages or e-mails.

♦ Include your scripted close every single time.

♦ See or talk to someone or do a review of your appointments from the day before.

## Getting Sales Without Leads
1. Open House Parties
2. Contact existing customers
3. Bulk neighborhood mailing
4. Canvassing/surveys
5. Door Hangers
6. Job Signs
7. Trade shows and events
8. Approach malls for rental space (kiosks or booths)
9. Silent salesman: Install sign up to win boxes at stores and restaurants.
10. Rehash (call back prospects that didn't buy)
11. Send special offers
12. Brochures/mailers/check on trade associations/groups/unions
13. Research mailing lists
14. Work your customers for referrals
15. Friends and Family Program
16. Open House at your office or showroom
17. Gift Certificates, Rebate Checks, Coupons

## Habits of Great Salespeople
1. Dress well
2. Be absolutely on time
3. Smile
4. Establish trust

**5.** Be enthusiastic

**6.** Be honest

**7.** Be confident

**8.** Be accountable

**9.** Relax

**10.** Use the customers' names

**11.** Establish your position

**12.** Ask the right questions

**13.** Don't waste their time

**14.** Know when to move into the presentation

**15.** Take the lead

**16.** Control the presentation

**17.** Isolate the need

**18.** Solve problems (issues)

**19.** Get feedback

**20.** Don't stereotype customers or objections

**21.** Engage the customer

**22.** Be a great 'listener'

**23.** Differentiate

**24.** Educate

**25.** Be tactful

**26.** Be patient

**27.** Don't 'close' too early

**28.** Cultivate the lead

**29.** Be a 'consultant'

**30.** Reset the one-legger or 'time close'

**31.** Take notes

**32.** Focus on solutions

**33.** Build a relationship

**34.** Sell yourself on yourself

**35.** Write your goals

**36.** Share your goals

**37.** Keep things in perspective

**38.** Start early

**39.** Make time for yourself

**40.** Read

**41.** Ask for the order

**42.** Assume the order

**43.** Send or e-mail a 'thank you'

**44.** Network with others

**45.** Help someone else

**46.** Believe in your company

**47.** Work towards your goals

**48.** Tell everyone where you work

**49.** Keep your sense of humor

**50.** Laugh with your customer

**51.** Think positive

**52.** Ask for referrals

**53.** Make More Money!

# About the Author

Rick's sales and marketing skills span 30 years. He has built a network of home improvement companies, increasing net sales by 30% yearly by developing, building and managing a sales force of 45 representatives.

He accomplished this by selling though telemarketing, acquiring contacts at shows and events as well as in field selling using a structured sales presentation through a unique but systematic approach.

Rick has received the following recognition:

• Named by Qualified Remodeler Magazine as a "Top 500 Remodeling Company" for ten straight years and "#1 Sunroom Specialty Remodeling Company" in 2003.

• Named by Replacement Contractor as a "Top 100 Home Improvement Company" for 10 years running.

• Recognized by national remodeling trade magazines for developing websites, brochures and advanced in-home remodeling sales presentations.

• Three, 3-year terms on the Board of Directors of the Better Business Bureau (BBB) of Western PA, 3 years as Board Chairman as well as a member of the committee to elect local bureau president.

• 10 years on the Board of Directors of National Association of the Remodeling Industry (NARI).

• Board of Directors, Juvenile Diabetes Research Foundation (JDRF).

• Board of Directors of the National Sunroom Association (NSA).

- - - - - - - - - - - - - - - - - - - - - - - - - - - - - - - - - - - - - - - -

# For more information
# on Rick Edwards'
# **Sell! Sell! Sell!**
# **Make More Money**
# System & Seminars:

**Visit <u>www.SellSellSellBook.com</u> now!!!**

# Dedications

**To my bother Jim,** such a great guy, we all miss him so much!

**To the salespeople and trainers** that taught me the simple selling structure...

**To the trainees who...**
♦ Put their confidence in what I know and the structure I teach
♦ Taught me what they know about selling
♦ Became selling superstars using a structured sales approach

**To my Dad...**
My Dad had a successful home improvement business when I was felt I was ready to start my sales career.

At that time, I was working in the installation end of the business for his best friend and ex-partner, Scott DeWitt, who was really good at the sales role, too! I wasn't shy about letting the sales pros know that I wanted to learn exactly how to 'sell'.

Scott DeWitt gave me a 3x5 card with a script for canvassing because he needed leads. This was my first memorized presentation for selling. My Dad had told me so much about how sales were made, who the superstars of the trade were and even how much money these guys made!

As I talked about actually starting a sales career it at such a young age, my Dad made it clear that he had a really good sales force and that he didn't want me blowing *his* leads.

He said it a little nicer than that, but I knew what he was saying! I had to find another way. Scott DeWitt actually suggested that I get in with a company that would give me a more formal education in sales.

Along came Rick Edwards at 19 years young as a sales applicant at Busy Beaver Remodelers, a premier home improvement company. After an interview with Murray Gross, vice president, who is still super-successful in the remodeling industry, the structured sales training started. Thank You!

# To be continued at...
## www.sellsellsellbook.com